Frederick Otto

The American Pastry Baker

General instructor in the baking of all kinds pastries, cakes & custards

Frederick Otto

The American Pastry Baker
General instructor in the baking of all kinds pastries, cakes & custards

ISBN/EAN: 9783741103087

Manufactured in Europe, USA, Canada, Australia, Japa

Cover: Foto ©Gila Hanssen / pixelio.de

Manufactured and distributed by brebook publishing software
(www.brebook.com)

Frederick Otto

The American Pastry Baker

THE

American Pastry Baker

OR

GENERAL INSTRUCTOR

In the Baking of all Kinds

PASTRIES, CAKES & CUSTARDS,

BY

FR. OTTO,

Practical Pastry Baker.

PUBLISHED BY

HOFFMAN & MORWITZ, 612 & 614 Chestnut Street,

PHILADELPHIA.

PREFACE

TO THE FIRST EDITION.

Induced by the growth of technical literature and the progress made in arts and trades as well as by special encouragement of several bakers, the Editor has made it his business, to issue this little book and thereby to assist with some valuable hints Master-bakers and their apprentices, giving them some useful informations in their trade.

The Editor has made it a point, to be as short as possible without loss to clearness and comprehensiveness, in order to make his subject easy understood and digested. His name is sufficient guarantee for the correctness of his receipts, he being generally known as a theoretically thoroughly versed and practically working baker since more than fifteen years, and having them used in his own business.

As this is the only work treating the manufacture of Pastry, which has made its appearance in print in America, it is to be hoped, that the same will meet with a favorable reception.

FR. OTTO.

CHAPTER I.

———

Treats of the various styles of Baking incidental to the business of the American Pastry Baker.

There are different kinds of dough, which, according to their component parts and method of preparing, may be classified as follows :

1. Puff paste.
2. Short paste.
3. Home made paste.
4. Common Short paste.

———

1. PUFF PASTE.

In the manufacture of good puff paste, sound butter and very fine flour are imperatively necessary. To

1 pound of flour, 1 pound of butter and 2 eggs must be added; the butter must be washed in fresh water, rounded to a strip about as thick as a finger, and left in water for several hours; in summer a piece of ice should be put into the water. Take the flour, ¼ pound of butter, the yellow part of an egg, stirred clear with a little rum, and a little very cold water, and knead it into a regular solid dough until it becomes almost as stiff as the butter, roll it out to the thickness of a finger, lay the butter (dry) in the middle, put the sides of the dough together over the butter, beat it gently with the roller, turn the dough and roll it, having first sprinkled it with very little flour, to a four-cornered slab of about a finger's thickness; then lay the sides over so that the edges meet, roll it even again and lay the dough once more together, so that it has now been folded four times.

The process just described is called the beating of the dough. It is then left to lay quietly for about ¼ hour, the same process repeated 2, 3, or 4 times, with a pause of about 10 or 15 minutes between each beating.

After the last beating the dough will be done and ready to be worked into every variety of baking. Care must be taken that the butter be neither too soft nor too hard. In the former case the dough will cling to the table when rolled out, and lose its smooth appearance; when baking, it will not raise any better than when the butter is too hard, and thereby loses its value. The dough will also lose its transparency and delicate gloss by sprinkling too much flour on it, when it is rolled out.

2. SHORT PASTE.

For the main stem take to 1 pound of flour $\frac{1}{2}$ pound of butter and the yolks of 8 eggs.

Another kind of short paste is made as follows: 1 pound of flour, $\frac{3}{4}$ pounds of butter, $\frac{1}{4}$ pound of sugar, the yolks of four eggs and 1 gill of water.

Receipt for a third kind of short paste: 1 pound of flour, $\frac{3}{4}$ pounds of butter, $\frac{1}{2}$ pound of finely ground almonds, $\frac{1}{4}$ pound of sugar, the yolks of 4 eggs, $\frac{1}{2}$ gill of sour cream, 1 lemon-peel grated and a litte ground cinnamon.

The butter must be hard, tough and well washed, and all the ingredients rapidly made to a dough, so that it becomes smooth and clear. If the dough is worked too long with warm hands, it becomes brittle and loses its smooth surface and tenacity, and is rendered useless for fine baking.

3. HOME MADE PASTE.

To 1 pound of flour take $\frac{3}{4}$ pounds of lard and 1 gill of water, in which $\frac{1}{4}$ ounce of salt should be dissolved, viz.: 4 pounds of flour, 3 pounds of lard, 1 ounce of salt and 1 pint of water.

Another receipt is: 1 pound of flour, $\frac{1}{2}$ pound of lard, $\frac{1}{4}$ ounce of salt, 1 gill of water; viz.: 4 pounds of flour, 2 pounds of lard, 1 ounce of salt and 1 pint of water.

4. COMMON SHORT PASTE.

To 1 pound of flour, 6 ounces of lard, $\frac{1}{4}$ ounce salt and 1 gill of water; viz.: 4 pounds of flour, $1\frac{1}{2}$ pounds of lard, 1 ounce of salt and 1 pint of water.

Another kind:—1 pound of flour, $\frac{1}{4}$ pound of lard, $\frac{1}{2}$ ounce of salt, $\frac{1}{2}$ pint of water; viz.: 4 pounds of flour, 1 pound of lard, 2 ounces of salt and 1 quart of water.

This last dough is used in many bakeries for the bottom crust, which is not advisable, as the pies become tough and unpalatable, although the top crust be made of other dough.

The last mentioned doughs, Nos. 2, 3 and 4, are prepared in the following manner: Flour and lard, or flour and butter, must be kneaded on the baking table or pan until a dough could be made of it without the addition of the water, but care must be taken that the mass does not become lumpy. A large hole is then made in the centre by drawing the mass apart and closing the edges well in, so that the water cannot trickle through and drop on the floor; pour water, in which the salt has already been dissolved, into it, draw the mass slowly from all sides under the water, and then rapidly make a dough of the whole without kneading the same too much. When making the Short Paste No. 2, the eggs must be beaten well together before being added to the dough. The lard as well as the butter must be stiff and hard. In winter, it generally must be warmed a little, but care must be taken that it does not get too soft, as the dough then will not become light. The pies should always be made in not too hot a place, and then, as soon as possible, baked in a hot, air-tight oven.

The edge of the bottom crust, after being put on the plate, must be washed with water, and several indentions made on the cover with the jagging iron, as the former prevents the juice of the fruit from oozing out of the pie while baking, and the latter, by giving outlet to the steam from the pies, prevents the cover from being raised, which makes them hollow and gives them a bad appearance. It is also better to break the dough just as it is needed for rolling, instead of breaking the whole batch in pieces at once, as it thereby loses in lightness.

The pies are generally washed with milk or with the beaten yolks of eggs and milk, which gives them a gloss and good color.

CHAPTER II.

Treats of the making of pies and tarts and their various fillings.

---

1. HOW TO MAKE PIES.

Break a piece of dough from the batch, about the size you require for a pie, roll it out and cover the plate with it, which process continue until all your plates are covered. Then fill them with any kind of marmelade, green or preserved fruits, and wash the edge of the lower crust with water; then roll out your cover (making the same process as with the lower crust), mark it and make an opening in it with the jagging iron or knife, lay it over the fruit and press the dough smooth on the edges of the plates, or cut it with a sharp knife; then wash the pies with milk, or yolks of eggs and milk, and bake them in a hot, air-tight oven.

2. HOW TO MAKE TARTS.

The cover generally consists of butter paste or short paste, and the fillings of slices, quarters, or eighths of apples, apricots, peaches, oranges, halves of plums, stoned cherries, strawberries, raspberries, gooseberries, marmelade, jelly, preserved fruits and cream. The fruit slices, strawberries, raspberries, etc. must, before being used for tarts, etc., for a while, be laid in fine sugar, grated lemon peel, or some other spice, or, according to circumstances, the former must be stewed, and the smaller fruits, excepting plums and cherries, which should be sprinkled with sugar before baking, should be stewed in sugar.

The tarts generally are covered with network. After the dough-covered plates have been filled with whatever fruit may be preferred, cut with your jagging iron long strips, about the width of a finger, from the dough, which should be rolled out flat about ⅛ of an inch thick, and plait these strips over the filling, laying the first one across the centre, the second crossing the first, then two others from each side of the first, then two from each side of the second, keeping them about $\frac{1}{4}$ of an inch apart, so that two strips alternately cross from side to side until the whole filling is covered, as it were, with a net work. The ends then must be cut off clean at the edges, the ridge of the tart washed with egg and then bordered with one of the before mentioned strips; wash the tarts with egg, but be careful that none of it runs off on the sides. Bake in a medium hot oven.

For very small tarts the strips must, of course, be made proportionally narrower, in order to make a net work on so small a surface.

All tarts of puff paste must be glazed well with pulverized sugar while in the oven, or else covered with snow of the white of eggs and sugar, sprinkled with water, and baked in a more than medium hot oven.

Small tarts generally are made in the following manner: Have your puff paste rolled out thin, press out the slices with your form, put them into the appropriate tin moulds, and then add your filling.

Or, after having rolled out your dough about $\frac{1}{4}$ inch thick, press out the under crust of about 3 or 4 inches diameter, put it on the baking pan, wash it with egg, and put on an edging of about ½ inch in height, put in your filling and proceed according to foregoing directions. This last kind of shell for tarts is used for Oyster Pattys, but is generally baked alone and filled afterwards.

---

3. ON THE PREPARATION OF THE VARIOUS FILLINGS.

1. MINCE PIE.

Take 5 pounds of beef and 10 pounds of apples chop fine, or prepare it with the machine, add 3 pounds raisins, 3 pounds currants, ½ pound citron, 5 pounds sugar, or three pounds sugar and 2 pints of the best molasses, 1 ounce of ground cloves, 1 ounce of ground clove pepper, ½ ounce of nutmeg and mix with 2 pints of good brandy and the meat broth, and then press the mass in a pot, (it will keep from 2 to 3 months in a cold but not damp place) and thin it when used with cider.

2. ANOTHER KIND OF MINCE PIE.

Take 6 pounds of beef from the loin, and scrape all the skin and sinews from it with a knife, cook a fresh beef tongue, and after removing the skin after it has become cold, chop it up with the loin of beef. Then chop 2 pounds of stoned raisins fine, clean and wash 4 pounds of currants, take 1 pound of sugar, 2 nutmegs, ½ ounce mace, 1 ounce ground cloves, 18 large pared and grated apples, a handfull of salt and 1 pint of Cognac, mix the ingredients well together and then press them into a box.

3. LEMON PIE.

Beat up ½ pound sugar with 12 eggs lightly, and stir the following articles in with them : ¼ pound of butter, the grated rinds and juice of 4 lemons, and 1 quart of water.

4. ANOTHER SORT OF LEMON PIE.

Beat up 4 eggs with ½ pound of sugar lightly, add the grated peel and juice of 3 lemons, then dissolve two ounces of corn-starch in a little cold water, and let it boil one minute in 1 quart of boiling water, stirring it all the time to prevent it from burning, and, after cooling a little, mix the above ingredients in.

5. APPLE PIE.

Cut one peck of apples and boil them soft in 4 quarts of water, add from 4 to 8 pounds of white sugar, and let simmer for half an hour; rub the same through a sieve, and season with cinnamon or nutmeg.

Or, peel and core the apples, and cut them in thin slices; then chop them fine, and mix them with some cinnamon, grated lemon-peel, chopped almonds, sugar, small raisins and wine.

6. PEACH PIE.

Stone the peaches and slice them thinly, fill the dishes and sweeten them with powdered sugar, adding a little water; instead of sugar and water some of the best molasses may be used.

You may also cut the peaches in eighths, adding pounded almonds, grated lemon-peel, some wine and sugar, but when the fruit is not very ripe, it would be preferable to boil the same first, however not more than half-soft and only in sufficient water to prevent burning. When cold enough remove the stones and sweeten with sugar at your pleasure.

7. PLUM PIE.

Do the same as with peaches.

8. RHUBARB PIE.

Take the tender sticks of rhubarb and after skinning them, cut them into short pieces and put them on the dough in the dishes, then sprinkle some grated lemon-peel on the top, also from 2 to 3 ounces of sugar on each dish, moisted with a little water, and strew some flour over all, before closing the top. When Rhubarb pies are made in this manner, they are to be baked at a star fire, because with too much heat the filling would not get properly soft. The most convenient and quickest way is, to cook the rhubarb previously; viz: Take for 8 pounds of prepared rhubarb 2 quarts of water and make it boil at a moderate fire, and add to it finally 6 to 8 pounds of white sugar and some grated lemon-peel. When the whole is boiling again, mix with it 1 ounce of corn starch dissolved in a little cold water and leave it on the fire a few minutes longer.

9. CHERRY PIE.

10. GOOSEBERRY PIE.

11. CURRANT PIE.

12. GRAPE PIE.

13. HUCKLEBERRY PIE.

14. BLACKBERRY PIE.

15. RASPBERRY PIE.

16. STRAWBERRY PIE.

These sundry eight pies are made in the same way. The fruit must be properly picked and all stalks, leaves etc. etc. thoroughly removed, then filled into the dishes containing the dough and covered with about 2 to 4 ounces of powdered sugar to each pie, some fruit requiring more sugar than others, especially gooseberries, the sugar to be moistened with a little water, and some flour to be sprinkled over before the top is put on.

Or you may cook the fruit first, by simmering slowly with little water and after adding the necessary sugar, leaving the same still from 5 to 10 minutes on the fire. To each pound of fruit, 1 to 2 gills of water and ½ to 1 pound of sugar are required.

17. RAISIN PIE.

Beat 1 pound of sugar and 12 eggs nicely together and mix into it 3 pounds of raisins, after having scalded the latter in 2 quarts of boiling water; then add some grated lemon-peel.

18. ANOTHER DESCRIPTION CF RAISIN PIE.

Boil 2 pounds of raisins in 2 quarts of water until they are soft, add 1 ounce of corn starch previously dissolved in a little cold water and let the whole cook for a few minutes. Beat 6 eggs and $\frac{3}{4}$ pound of sugar nicely together adding some grated lemon-peel.

19. ANOTHER RAISIN PIE.

Scald the raisins in boiling water and fill therewith the dishes already covered with the paste. Pour some of the best molasses on, add the grated lemon-peel and sprinkle with flour before covering with paste.

20. QUINCE PIE

The pared quinces are to be cooked in wine or good cider, with sugar and cinnamon, lemon-peel and some cloves. until reduced to a marmelade, press this mass through a sieve and spread it on the top and close the pies.

21. ORANGE PIE.

Boil 2 pounds of pared and cored apples with $\frac{1}{2}$ pound of sugar, 2 ounces of pulverized almonds and $\frac{1}{2}$ pint of wine, until they become a marmelade, which you put on the paste in the dishes. Then grate the peel of 2 or 3 oranges, take the skin off and cut them into thin slices; spread these on the apple marmelade and the grated peel on the top. Cover up.

22. MARLBOROUGH PIE.

Beat 4 eggs and 1 pound of sugar together up in 1 quart of milk, add 4 pounds of apple marmelade and a little nutmeg, fill the dishes, put the top on and bake as usual.

23. CREAM PIE.

Put 1 quart of white wine with 1 pound of sugar on the fire. Beat in a pitcher the yolks of 8 and the white of 2 eggs, add 1 ounce of corn starch, dissolved in a little cold water and the grated peel of 1 lemon. The eggs ought to be well beaten up and poured into the wine, when it is boiling, and the stirring must be continued without interruption until the mixture is boiling again. When cool, to be filled into the dishes without delay and to be baked as usual.

24. VANILLA CREAM PIE.

Pound 1 stick of vanilla quite fine, pour 1 quart of white wine thereon, add 8 whole eggs, $\frac{1}{2}$ pound of sugar and 1 oz. of corn-starch dissolved in a little cold water. Put on coal-fire and turn quickly until boiling, then remove it immediately from the fire, stirring the cream until it gets cold, and finish the pies in the usual manner.

25. GOOSELIVER PIE.

Six large white gooselivers well larded with the fine cut fat of pickled pork and fresh truffles to be seasoned with salad oil, powdered spice and lemon juice. Take $\frac{1}{2}$ pound of truffles, $\frac{1}{2}$ pound of boiled veal and the breasts of some chickens, $\frac{1}{2}$ pound of fat pork and some charlottes, chop all together very fine, beat $\frac{1}{2}$ pound of butter with 2 eggs and mix all these last named ingredients together, adding some salt and 1 pint of beeftea. Mix well and let stand.

Cover a dish with pie crust, sprinkling the same with parmesan cheese, and spread half the mixture thereon, then put the larded gooseliver and on the top the other half of the mixture again. Cover with thin slices of salt pork and then with the crust. Give it a coat of the yolk of eggs and bake. This pie has an excellent flavor.

26. GOOSELIVER IMITATION PIE.

2 pounds of veal from the haunch, ½ pound of new pickled pork, part of a smoked oxtongue boiled, or some ham, 1 ounce of boned and watered sardelles, 2 tablespoons full of capers, the flesh and peel of 1 lemon, to be chopped fine and mixed together. Season with cardamon, mace, cloves and pepper, adding 4 spoonfulls of wine. Fill with this mixture and bake.

27. EEL PATTIES.

The outside consists of puff paste. The clean flesh of a well grown eel is cut into thin well rounded pieces and these, after being pickled, are stiffened in butter, fine spices and lemon juice.

Of all the odd and ends of the fish, herb butter, sardelle butter, parmesan cheete, a good deal of thick and rich brown gravy and wheaten bread crumbs a fine stuffing is made, which must be soft enough to dissolve on your Tongue. The dough rolled out to a thickness of ¼ of an inch is to be cut by a circular form into underlayers of about 6 inches diameter. These receive a coat of eggs and round the outer edge a border half an inch high. Put some of the stuffing inside, a slice of eel theron and covered with stuffing again, to give it a hilly shape. Spread some parmesan cheese on the top, taking care, that none thereof falls on the surrounding border, sprinkle with lobster or crabfish paste or butter, paint the boarder crust with egg carefully, and bake the patties in a strong heat. These patties may also be made in crust top and bottom.

28. OYSTER PATTIES.

The outside consists of puff paste, and as to the rest proceed as before.

The extremely fine stuffing is mixed with the well boiled juice of the oysters left from the oysters, which have been stiffened in Rhinewine. Instead of this stuffiug, as advised for the eel patties, another may be substituted made of ground breadcrumbs, finely chopped herbs, sardelle butter, a few eggs, butter and some Rhinewine. Put into the stuffing of each patty three shaved oysters. These patties also can be made with top and bottom crust.

29. CRABFISH PATTIES.

Take puff paste, thinly rolled out, and cover small patty dishes, and prepare the outside in the same way as for eel patties. Mix $1\frac{1}{2}$ quarts of milk with 4 eggs, which have been stirred on the fire into one mass with 2 spoonfulls of flour, a good $\frac{1}{4}$ pound of crabfish, butter, 2 ounces of sugar and some nutmeg. When cold, add the yolks of 6 eggs and ultimately the white of 4 eggs beaten up. Put into each dish half a spoonfull of crab hash, cover with parmesan cheese and crabfish butter and fill up with the mass described above.

30. CRANBERRY PIE.

Boil one pound of cranberries in one pint of water until soft, add one pound of fine white sugar and let simmer from 15 to 20 minutes.

Another kind of Cranberry Pie is made by boiling one pound of cranberries in one quart of water, until soft, and one pound of sugar and by adding one ounce of corn starch dissolved in a little cold water. Let boil 1 to 2 minutes more and then remove from the fire.

31. APRICOT PIE.

Peel and stone 2 pounds of apricots, quarter them. Take one ounce of grated sweet almonds, $\frac{1}{2}$ ounce of bitter almonds, ¼ pound of sugar, ¼ ounce of citron, the grated peel of one lemon, ½ ounce of allspice and sufficient gelatine to make the mixture form a jelly. Cook it all together and when cold fill your pie dishes and bake as usual.

32. PINE APPLE PIE.

Remove the outside from the pine-apple and cut it into thin slices, which you mix in a kettle with sugar, grated lemon peel, ground cinnamon and some Rhinewine. Cook a short time over a slow fire, before filling the pie crust.

33. LEMON CREAM PIE.

Mix the yolk of 10 eggs with one ounce of flour or corn starch, the juice and grated peel of four lemons, ½ pound of sugar, 4 ounces of powdered almonds including one ounce of bitter ones, 2 ounces of citron, a little cardamon, ½ pint of Rhinewine and a pinch of salt. Put it on the fire and stirr until the mixture becomes quite hot and begins thickening and then add the beaten-up white of half the number of eggs.

34 PIES OF DRIED FRUIT.

All sorts of dried fruit, such as peaches, apples, New York plums, prunes, etc., are to be soaked a good while in cold water first and afterwards cooked soft on a starfire. Drive through a sieve, add the necessary sugar and let boil until all the water is fully absorbed and the fruit has the appearance of apple butter.

CHAPTER III.

CUSTARDS.

GENERAL REMARKS.

For custards use new laid eggs only and cook the custard only in a kettle, standing inside of a vessel filled with boiling water.

1. BOILED CUSTARD.

Boil one quart of milk with some sticks of cinnamon and a little lemon peel. Sweeten with $1\frac{1}{2}$ pounds of fine white sugar, scum it and when moderately cool, add gradually 8 well beaten eggs and some rosewater. Stir the whole on a slow fire and when thickening pour into cups or glasses.

2. ANOTHER DESCRIPTION.

Take the yolk of 10 eggs and the white of four. Beat the same slightly with ½ pound of sugar and pour it gradually in a quart of milk, which is nearly boiling. Add some rosewater and stir the whole on a slow fire until it has the required thickness. Then fill the cups and glasses, spread the beaten froth of the remaining white of 6 eggs over the top and fine powdered sugar thereon and glace the surface by holding a hot iron above it.

3. COMMON CUSTARD.

Boil 1 quart of milk with some sticks of cinnamon and lemon-peel. Dissolve 1 ounce of cornstarch in a little cold milk and let the boiled milk run through a sieve thereon, then add gradually the well beaten yolk of 6 eggs. Put the whole on a slow fire and stir until the proper consistency is obtained, then fill the cups or glasses and give them a sprinkling of fine sugar and nutmeg.

4. RICE CUSTARD.

Mix 1 pint of milk, 1 pint of cream, 1 ounce of sifted rice-meal, some rosewater, ¼ pound of sugar

and stir above the fire until the mixture begins to
boil; or you may boil two pounds of good clean rice
in 1 quart of milk; let it become quite soft, add the
well beaten yolk of 4 eggs and allow it to boil a few
minutes under constant stirring. Fill your cups
and sift some fine sugar and nutmeg on the top.

5. BAKED CUSTARD.

Beat lightly 12 eggs with ¾ pound of sugar and
add gradually under constant stirring 2 quarts of
milk, also some nutmeg and rosewater, or cinnamon
and grated lemon-peel. Cover the dishes with dough,
put them into the oven and fill them, but not more
than three at the time, or the dough in the dishes
would blister, before they could be filled.

6. ANOTHER SORT.

Boil 2 quarts of milk with a little cinnamon and
lemon-peel. Dissolve 4 ounces of corn-starch in
about one pint of cold milk and pour the boiled milk
through a sieve over it under continual stirring and
add furthermore 2 quarts of cold milk in the same
way. Whisk 12 eggs lightly with one pound of
sugar, and while constantly beating, let all the milk
slowly run into it. Continue the whisking of the
whole for some time, and bake as explained before.

7. COCOANUT CUSTARD.

Beat 12 eggs with one pound of sugar nicely, stir into it from 2 to 4 ounces of melted and clarified butter, a peeled and rounded cocoanut, add slowly 2 quarts of milk. Whisk the whole for a while and bake as usual.

8. ANOTHER KIND.

Beat 16 eggs with one pound of sugar nicely and slowly, add 1 grated cocoanut, $\frac{1}{4}$ pound of butter and 2 quarts of milk. Soak 2 to 3 pounds of bread in 2 quarts of milk, rub it through a sieve and add it to the above. Stir all together for a few minutes and bake the custards in the customary manner. This mass is especially adapted for the small cocoanut patties.

9. PUMPKIN CUSTARD.

Cut a pumpkin into pieces, removing the rind and seed, and boil 8 pounds thereof quite soft. Throw it into a sieve and let all the water run off. Then rub it through the sieve into some earthen vessel, and add $\frac{1}{4}$ pound of butter, $\frac{1}{2}$ ounce of salt, 2 ounces of ground ginger, a little grated lemon-peel and 3 quarts of milk. Stir well. Beat 18 eggs and $1\frac{1}{2}$ pounds of sugar nicely together. Mix all the ingredients together and bake as usual.

10. SWEET-POTATOE CUSTARD.

Boil 4 pounds of sweet-potatoes, but carefully avoid deseased ones, as one of the latter would spoil the flavor of the rest. Peel them and force them through a sieve. Add $\frac{1}{4}$ pound of butter, some cinnamon and 2 quarts of milk, also 8 eggs beaten up with $\frac{1}{2}$ pound of sugar. Beat the whole of it for another few minutes and proceed as with the previously named custards.

11. CHEESE CUSTARD.

Soak 1 pound of bread in 1 quart of milk and press the same with 4 pounds of sweet cheese through a sieve. Whisk very lightly 12 eggs and 1 pound of sugar, adding gradually 2 quarts of milk. Stir all well together, season with some cinnamon, grated lemon-peel and some rosewater, and bake the custard in the accustomed fashion.

INDEX.

CHAPTER I.

CHAPTER II.

CHAPTER III.

CUSTARDS.

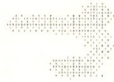

Der Amerikanische

Pasteten-Bäcker

oder

Instruktive Anweisung

zur Anfertigung aller Arten

Pasteten, Torten & Eierrahme,

von

Fr. Otto,

Praktischer Pasteten-Bäcker.

Verlag von

Hoffman & Morwitz,

Philadelphia.

1872.

Vorwort

zur ersten Auflage.

———

Bei dem Wachsen der technischen Literatur und den Fortschritten in Kunst und Gewerben, sowie durch besondere Veranlassung mehrerer Bäcker, hat es sich der Verfasser zur Aufgabe gemacht, dieses kleine Buch herauszugeben und so allen geneigten Abnehmern, besonders den Herren Bäckermeistern und deren Lehrlingen, lehrreich an die Hand zu gehen und ihnen manchen Vortheil für ihr Geschäft zu bieten.

Der Verfaſſer hat ſich hauptſächlich bemüht, ſich ſo kurz wie möglich, und doch klar und deutlich, darin auszudrücken, und ſomit Allen das Ganze leicht begreiflich und verſtändlich zu machen. Für die Zuverläſſigkeit ſeiner Recepte bürgt ſein Name, welcher als tüchtiger und praktiſcher Bäcker ſchon länger als fünfzehn Jahre bekannt iſt, und hat derſelbe ſie in ſeinem eigenen Geſchäfte angewendet.

Da dieſes das einzige Werkchen iſt, welches hier in Amerika zur Anfertigung der hieſigen Pastryworks herausgegeben iſt, darf ich hoffen, daß daſſelbe eine günſtige Aufnahme finden wird.

Fr. Otto.

Erstes Kapitel.

Von den verschiedenen, im Geschäfte des amerikanischen Pastetenbäckers vorkommenden Backwerken.

Es giebt verschiedene Teigarten, und die man ihren materiellen Bestandtheilen und ihrer Zusammensetzungsart nach etwa auf folgende Weise klassificiren kann:

1. Blätterteig (puff paste.)
2. Mürberteig (short paste.)
3. Familienteig (home made paste.)
4. Gewöhnlicher Mürberteig (common short paste.)

---

1. Der Blätterteig (puff paste).

Zur Bereitung eines guten Blätterteigs ist feste, gute Butter und ganz feines Mehl eine unerläßliche Bedingung. Bei diesem Teige rechnet man auf's Pfund Mehl

ein Pfund Butter und zwei Eier. Man wäscht die
Butter in ganz frischem Wasser, knetet sie recht klar zu
einer daumesdicken Platte und läßt sie noch mehrere
Stunden in kaltem Wasser stehen, in welches man im
Sommer wo möglich ein Stück Eis legt. Von dem
Mehl, ¼ Pfund Butter, dem mit etwas Rum klargerühr=
ten Eigelb und etwas recht kaltem Wasser, knetet man
einen ausgeglichenen und so festen Teig, daß er beinahe
die Steifheit der Butter besitzt, rollt ihn fingerdick aus,
legt die abgetrocknete Butterplatte in die Mitte der Teig=
platte, schlägt den an den Seiten freigebliebenen Teig
über die Butter zusammen, klopft ihn mit dem Welger
leicht an, dreht den Teig um und rollt ihn, nachdem man
ganz wenig Mehl untergestreut hat, zu einer fingerdicken,
länglich viereckigen Platte aus. Man schlägt nun die
schmalen Seiten über einander, so daß sich die beiden
Kanten gegenseitig berühren, rollt sie mit dem Welger
glatt und schlägt den Teig noch einmal zusammen, so
daß er nun vierfach über einander liegt.

Dieses Verfahren, wie es hier beschrieben worden,
nennt man das Schlagen des Teiges. Man läßt ihn
nun eine Viertelstunde lang ruhig liegen, wiederholt das=
selbe Verfahren zwei, drei oder vier Mal mit einer jedes=
maligen Pause von 10 bis 15 Minuten nach dem er=
folgten Schlagen.

Wenn das letzte Schlagen erfolgt ist, dann ist der
Teig fertig, und nun verarbeitet man ihn zu allerlei

Backwerken. Man hüte sich dabei vor zu weicher wie zu
harter Butter. Bei der ersten klebt der Teig bei dem
Ausrollen auf dem Tische fest und verliert dadurch sein
glattes Ansehen; er geht bei dem Backen ebenso wenig
auf, als der von zu harter Butter, und hat dann seinen
Werth verloren. Ebenso verliert der Teig seine schöne
Durchsichtigkeit und zarte Glätte, wenn bei dem Aus=
rollen zu viel Mehl untergestreut wird.

2. Mürber Teig (short paste).

Zum Hauptstamm kommen auf ein Pfund Mehl ein
halbes Pfund Butter und 8 Eidotter.

Zu einem andern mürben Teige nimmt man auf ein
Pfund Mehl ¾ Pfund Butter, ¼ Pfund Zucker, 4 Ei=
dotter und 1 Gill Wasser.

Ein anderer mürber Teig wird bereitet von 1 Pfund
Mehl, ¾ Pfund Butter, ½ Pfund feingestoßenen Man=
deln, ¼ Pfund Zucker, 8 Eidottern, ½ Gill saurem Rahm,
der abgeriebenen Schale einer Citrone und etwas gesto=
ßenem Zimmt.

Die Butter muß hart und zähe und gut ausgewaschen
sein, auch müssen alle Zuthaten schnell zu einem Teige
vereinigt werden, damit letzterer schön glatt und klar
bleibe. Bleibt der Teig durch anhaltendes Wirken lange
unter den warmen Händen, so wird er brüchig, verliert
seine glatte Außenseite und Bindekraft und ist zu keiner
Art von feinem Backwerk mehr zu gebrauchen.

3. Familienteig (home made paste).

Auf 1 Pfund Mehl kommt ¾ Pfund Schmalz und 1 Gill Wasser, worin ¼ Unze Salz aufgelöst ist; z. B. 4 Pfund Mehl, 3 Pfund Schmalz, 1 Unze Salz und 1 Pint Wasser.

Zu einem andern Teige nimmt man zu einem Pfunde Mehl ½ Pfund Schmalz, ¼ Unze Salz und 1 Gill Wasser; z. B. 4 Pfund Mehl, 2 Pfund Schmalz, 1 Unze Salz und 1 Pint Wasser.

4. Gewöhnlicher Mürber Teig (common short paste).

Auf ein Pfund Mehl nimmt man 6 Unzen Schmalz, ¼ Unze Salz und 1 Gill Wasser; z. B. 4 Pfund Mehl, 1½ Pfund Schmalz, 1 Unze Salz und 1 Pint Wasser.

Zu einem andern Teige nimmt man auf 1 Pfund Mehl ¼ Pfund Schmalz, ½ Unze Salz, ½ Pint Wasser, z. B. 4 Pfund Mehl, 1 Pfund Schmalz, 2 Unzen Salz und 1 Quart Wasser.

Dieser letzte Teig wird in vielen Bäckereien zu Boden= kruste verwendet, doch ist derselbe nicht zu empfehlen, weil die Pies zu zähe werden und sich nicht gut essen lassen, obgleich die obere Kruste von mürberem Teige ist.

Die letzten Teigarten, unter No. 2, 3 und 4, werden auf folgende Weise bereitet: Mehl und Schmalz, oder Mehl und Butter, reibt man auf der Backtafel oder in

der Backschüssel mit den Händen so lange leicht zusam=
men, bis man einen Teig davon machen könnte, ohne
daß das Wasser hinzu gemischt würde, aber die Masse
darf sich dennoch nicht zusammen ballen. Nun macht man in der Mitte ein weites Loch, indem
man die Masse auseinander schiebt, die Außenseite rings=
um gut fest andrückt, damit das Wasser nicht durch=
brechen und auf den Boden laufen kann; gießt das
Wasser, in welchem schon das Salz aufgelöst ist, hinein,
zieht die Masse langsam von allen Seiten unter das
Wasser ein und vereinigt alles schnell zu einem Teige,
ohne denselben viel zu bearbeiten. Bei dem mürben
Teige No. 2 müssen die Eier erst gut zusammen zerquirlt
werden, ehe sie zu dem Teige kommen. Das Schmalz
muß ebenfalls wie die Butter recht steif und hart sein,
im Winter muß man es gewöhnlich etwas wärmen, wo=
bei man sich aber hüte, dasselbe zu weich werden zu
lassen, weil die Kruste sonst nicht locker wird. Die Pa=
steten sollten stets an einem nicht zu heißen Orte zube=
reitet und dann sobald wie möglich in einem heißen und
luftdichten Ofen gebacken werden. Der Rand der Bo=
denkruste, nachdem die Teller damit belegt sind, muß mit
Wasser abgewaschen und in den Deckel einige Schnitte
mit dem Backrad (jagging iron) gemacht werden. Er=
steres verhindert, daß der Saft der Früchte während des
Backens herausläuft, und letzteres läßt den Dampf aus
den Pasteten und verhütet dadurch, daß der Deckel sich in

die Höhe hebt, wodurch die Pasteten hohl und ein
schlechtes Aussehen bekommen würden. Auch ist es
besser, wenn man von dem Teige ein Stück nach dem
andern abzupft, gerade wie man es zum Ausrollen ge=
braucht, anstatt daß man den ganzen Teig in Stücke
ausbricht, weil dadurch der Teig an Mürbheit verliert.
Gewöhnlich werden die Pasteten mit Milch oder mit ge=
schlagenen Eidottern und Milch abgewaschen, wodurch
sie eine schönere Farbe und schöneren Glanz erhalten.

Zweites Kapitel.

Von der Zubereitung der Pasteten und Torten und ihren verschiedenen Füllungen.

---

1. Von der Zubereitung der Pasteten.

Zupfe ein Stück von der Größe, wie Du es für die Pastete gebrauchst, von dem Teige ab, rolle es aus, belege damit den Teller und fahre so fort, bis alle Teller belegt sind; dann fülle sie mit irgend einer beliebigen Marmelade, grünen oder eingemachten Früchten, und wasche den Rand der Bodenkruste mit Wasser ab. Nun rolle den Deckel aus (verfahre dabei wie bei der Bodenkruste), zeichne ihn und schneide mit dem Backrade oder Messer eine kleine Oeffnung in denselben, lege ihn auf die Früchte und drücke den Teig am Rande des Tellers mit den Händen schön glatt ab, oder schneide ihn glatt ab

mit einem scharfen Messer, wasche die Pasteten mit Milch
oder gequirlten Eidottern und Milch, und backe sie in
einem heißen und luftdichten Ofen gar.

——

**2. Von der Zubereitung der Torten
(tarts).**

Die Teighülle besteht gewöhnlich aus Butterteig oder
mürbem Teig, und die Füllung aus den Scheiben, Vier=
teln und Achteln von Aepfeln, Aprikosen, Pfirsichen,
Apfelsinen, halben Pflaumen, ausgesteinten Kirschen,
Erdbeeren, Himbeeren, Stachelbeeren, auch Marmelade,
Jelly, eingemachten Früchten und Rahm. Die Frucht=
scheiben, auch die Erdbeeren, Himbeeren u. s. w., müssen
vor dem Auflegen eine Zeit lang in feinem Zucker, ab=
geriebener Citronenschale - oder anderen Würzen gelegen
haben, oder nach Umständen die ersteren etwas ange=
schmort und die übrigen kleinen Früchte, außer Pflaumen
und Kirschen, die man vor dem Backen nur mit Zucker
bestreut, in Zucker geschmort werden.

Die Torten werden gewöhnlich mit einem Gitter über=
flochten. Nachdem die mit Teig belegten Teller mit
irgend einer beliebigen Frucht ausgefüllt sind, schneidet
man mit dem Backrad lange, fingerbreite Streifen von
dem flach (⅓ Zoll dicken) ausgerollten Teige und flechtet
diese Streifen über das Füllsel, so daß man den ersten

Faden recht in die Mitte legt, einen andern quer über diesen zieht, dann zwei andere von jeder Seite des ersten Grundfadens, und wieder zwei andere von jeder Seite des zweiten Grundfadens, allemal einen Viertelzoll breit von einander abstehend darauflegt, und so von je zwei zu zwei Faden über das Kreuz wechselseitig fortfährt, bis das ganze Füllsel gitterartig überflochten ist. Dann schneidet man die Streifen dicht am Rande ab, bestreicht den Rand mit Ei, legt zunächst ein ebenso breites Band darauf, wäscht die Torten mit Ei, verhüte aber, daß nichts an den Seiten überfließt, und backt die Torten in mittelmäßiger Hitze gar.

Bei den kleinen Törtchen müssen natürlich auch die Streifen schmäler sein, um auf dem geringen Flächenraum ein kleines, einfaches Geflecht anzubringen. Alle Butterteig-Torten müssen mit feingestoßenem Zucker im Ofen recht blank glacirt werden, oder man bedeckt sie mit weichem Eiweißschnee und Zucker, bespritzt sie mit Wasser und backt sie in mehr als mittelmäßiger Hitze gar.

Die kleinen Torten (small tarts) werden gewöhnlich auf folgende Weise bereitet: Man sticht von dünn ausgerolltem Blätterteig mit einem Ausstecher kleine Scheiben aus, legt sie in die dazu passenden blechernen Förmchen und füllt sie mit irgend einer beliebigen Füllung. Oder man sticht von dem zu etwa $\frac{1}{4}$ Zoll dick ausgerollten Teige Boden von 3 bis 4 Zoll im Durch=

messer aus, legt sie auf das Backblech, bestreicht sie mit Ei, umgiebt die äußere Oberfläche mit einem schmalen, ½ Zoll hohen Kranze, füllt in die Mitte die Füllung und verfährt weiter damit, wie oben angegeben ist. Diese letzten kleinen Tortenhüllen nimmt man für die kleinen Oyster patty, werden aber meistens blind gebacken und nachher gefüllt.

---

3. Von der Bereitung der verschiedenen Füllungen.

1. Fleischpastete (Minced Pie).

Man hackt 5 Pfund gekochtes Rindfleisch mit 10 Pfund Aepfeln fein zusammen, oder thut es mit der Maschine, und nimmt 3 Pfund Rosinen, 3 Pfund Corinthen, ½ Pfund Citronat, 5 Pfund Zucker, oder 3 Pfund Zucker und 1 Quart von dem besten Molasses, 1 Unze gemahlene Nelken, 1 Unze gemahlenen Nelkenpfeffer, ½ Unze Muskatblüthen, mischt alles mit einem Quart guten Brandy und der Fleischbrühe zusammen, sodann drückt man die Masse in einen Topf (sie conservirt sich 2 bis 3 Monate an einem kühlen, aber nicht feuchten Orte) und verdünnt sie erst, wenn sie gebraucht wird, mit Cider.

2. Eine andere Art Minced Pies.

Man nehme 6 Pfund Rindslende, schabe sie mit einem Messer fein ab, damit weder Haut noch Sehnenfasern darin bleiben, koche eine frische Rindszunge, schäle die Haut davon ab und hacke sie dann nach dem Erkalten recht zart unter die geschabte Rindslende. Man hacke ferner 2 Pfund große, ausgekernte Rosinen, ebenfalls zart, lese und wasche 4 Pfund Corinthen, nehme 1 Pfund Zucker, 2 Muskatnüsse, ½ Unze Muskatblüthen, 1 Unze Nelken, zusammen gestoßen, 18 große, geschälte und auf einem Reibeisen geriebene Aepfel, eine Hand voll Salz und ½ Quart Cognac, mische alles gut zusammen und drücke die Masse in eine Büchse.

3. Citronenpastete (Lemon Pie).

Schlage ½ Pfund Zucker mit 12 Eiern leicht, rühre ¼ Pfund Butter, die abgeriebene Rinde und den Saft von 4 Citronen und 1 Quart Wasser dazu.

4. Eine andere Art Lemon pie.

Schlage 4 Eier mit ½ Pfund Zucker leicht und thue die abgeriebene Rinde und den Saft von 3 Citronen dazu, löse 2 Unzen Cornstarch in ein wenig kaltem Wasser auf und laß sie in 1 Quart kochendem Wasser eine Minute lang bei stetem Umrühren aufkochen, damit sie nicht anbrennt, und nachdem sie etwas abgekühlt ist, mische alles zusammen.

5. Apfelpastete (Apple pie).

Zerschneide 1 Peck Aepfel und koche sie in 4 Quart Wasser weich, setze dann 4 bis 8 Pfund weißen Zucker hinzu und laß sie noch ½ Stunde langsam kochen, reibe sie durch ein Sieb oder Durchschlag, und würze sie mit Zimmt oder Muskatnuß.

Oder schäle die Aepfel, nimm die Kerne heraus und schneide sie in dünne Scheiben, oder hacke sie in dünne Stückchen, und vermische sie dann in einer Schüssel mit etwas Zimmt, abgeriebener Citronenschale, kleingehackten Mandeln, Zucker, kleinen Rosinen und Wein.

6. Pfirsichpastete (Peach pie).

Nimm die Steine aus den Pfirsichen und schneide die letzteren in dünne Scheiben, fülle die Platten, streue Zucker darüber und gieße ein wenig Wasser dazu; auch kann man anstatt Zucker und Wasser von dem besten Molasses nehmen.

Ferner kann man die in Achtel zerschnittenen Pfirsiche zuerst in einer Schüssel mit kleingehackten Mandeln, abgeriebener Citronenschale, etwas Wein und Zucker vermischen. Wenn dieselben noch nicht recht reif sind, so ist es vortheilhafter, dieselben erst zu kochen, jedoch nur

halb weich und mit nur Wasser genug, daß sie nicht an=
brennen. Sobald sie kalt genug sind, nimm die Steine
heraus und süße sie mit Zucker nach Belieben.

7. Pflaumenpaftete (Plum pie).

Dieselbe wird wie Pfirsichpaftete bereitet.

8. Rhabarberpaftete (Rhubarb pie).

Nimm die zarten Halme des Rhabarber, und nachdem
die Haut abgezogen ist, schneide denselben in kurze Stück=
chen, fülle die mit Teig belegten Teller damit aus, streue
auf jede Paftete ein wenig abgeriebene Citronenschale,
2 bis 3 Unzen Zucker, netze denselben mit etwas Wasser
an und siebe ein wenig Mehl darüber, ehe der Deckel
daraufgelegt wird. Wenn Rhabarberpafteten auf diese
Weise bereitet werden, so muß man sie in schwacher
Hitze backen, weil bei zu starker Hitze die Füllung nicht
weich genug wird. Die bequemste und schnellste Art ist,
wenn man den Rhabarber zuerst kocht; z. B.: Nimm
zu 8 Pfund zubereiteten Rhabarber 2 Quart Wasser
und bringe ihn bei gelindem Feuer zum Sieden; thue
dann 6 bis 8 Pfund weißen Zucker und abgeriebene Ci=
ronenschale dazu. Wenn die Masse wieder im Kochen
ist, so gieße 1 Unze in ein wenig kaltem Wasser aufge=
löste Cornstarch hinzu und laß alles zusammen noch
einige Minuten kochen.

9. Kirschenpastete (Cherry pie).

10. Stachelbeerenpastete (Gooseberry pie).

11. Johannisbeerenpastete (Current pie).

12. Traubenpastete (Grape pie).

13. Heidelbeerenpastete (Huckleberry pie).

14. Brombeerenpastete (Blackberry pie).

15. Himbeerenpastete (Raspberry pie).

16. Erdbeerenpastete (Strawberry pie).

Alle diese acht Sorten Pasteten werden auf gleiche Weise zubereitet. Man zupfe von den Früchten die Stiele und die Butzen rein ab und lese die Früchte recht sauber aus, sodann fülle man dieselben in die mit Teig belegten Teller, streue Zucker darüber, ungefähr 2 bis 4 Unzen auf jede Pastete gerechnet — denn einige Sorten Früchte erfordern mehr Zucker wie die andern, z. B. Stachelbeeren — netze den Zucker mit etwas Wasser an und siebe ein wenig Mehl darüber, ehe der obere Deckel darauf gelegt wird.

Auch kann man alle diese Früchte zuerst kochen; bringe sie mit nur wenig Wasser langsam zum Sieden, setze den Zucker hinzu und lasse sie noch 5 bis 10 Minuten mit demselben kochen. Auf 1 Pfund dieser Früchte rechnet man 1 bis 2 Gill Wasser und $\frac{1}{2}$ bis 1 Pfund Zucker.

17. Rosinenpastete (Raisin pie).

Schlage 1 Pfund Zucker und 12 Eier leicht zusammen und rühre 3 Pfund Rosinen, welche mit 2 Quart kochendem Wasser angebrüht waren, nebst etwas abgeriebener Citronenschale dazu.

18. Eine andere Art Raisin pie.

Koche zwei Pfund Rosinen mit 2 Quart Wasser weich, gieße 1 Unze in etwas kaltem Wasser aufgelöste Cornstarch dazu und laß dieses noch einige Minuten aufkochen. Schlage 6 Eier und ¾ Pfund Zucker leicht, und rühre alles nebst etwas abgeriebener Citronenschale zusammen.

19. Eine andere Art Raisin pie.

Brühe die Rosinen mit kochendem Wasser an und fülle die mit Teig belegten Teller damit aus, gieße etwas vom besten Molasses dazu, abgeriebene Citronenschale, und siebe etwas Mehl darüber, ehe der Deckel darauf gelegt wird.

20. Quittenpastete (Quince pie).

Man kocht die geschälten Quitten zu einer Marmelade mit Wein oder gutem Apfelwein, Zucker und Zimmt, Citronenschale und etwas Nelken, reibt sie durch einen Durchschlag und füllt diese Masse in die mit Teig belegten Teller und streut noch etwas gehackte Mandeln darüber, ehe der Deckel darauf gelegt wird.

21. Apfelsinen= oder Pomeranzen=Pastete (Orange pie.)

Koche 2 Pfund geschälte und von Kernen befreite Aepfel mit ½ Pfund Zucker, zwei Unzen feingestoßenen Mandeln und ½ Pint Wein zu einer Marmelade, und fülle sie in die mit Teig belegten Teller. Ferner nehme man 2 oder 3 Orangen, reibe deren Schale ab, schäle dieselben nachher, schneide sie in dünne Scheiben, lege sie auf das ausgefüllte Aepfelmark und streue die abgeriebene Schale darüber und lege dann den Deckel darauf.

22. Marlborough Pie.

Man zerquirlt 4 Eier und 1 Pfund Zucker in 1 Quart Milch und mischt 4 Pfund Aepfelmarmelade nebst etwas Muskatnuß hinzu, füllt die mit Teig belegten Teller damit aus, legt den Deckel darüber und backt die Pastete wie gewöhnlich.

23. Rahmpastete (Cream pie).

Man setzt 1 Quart weißen Wein mit 1 Pfund Zucker auf das Feuer, schlägt in einen Topf 6 Eidotter und 2 ganze Eier, fügt 1 Unze Cornstarch, in etwas kaltem Wasser aufgelöst, und die abgeriebene Schale einer Citrone hinzu. Man zerquirlt die Eier gut, und wenn der Wein kocht, schüttet man die Eier unter stetem Quirlen in denselben und fährt damit so lange fort, bis der Rahm wieder am Kochen ist. Wenn derselbe abgekühlt ist, wird er sofort in die Pasteten gefüllt, und werden dieselben gebacken wie gewöhnlich.

24. Vanille-Rahmpastete (Vanille Cream pie).

Stoße eine Schote Vanille ganz fein, übergieße sie mit einem Quart weißen Wein, rühre 8 ganze Eier und ½ Pfund Zucker dazu, nebst 1 Unze Cornstarch, in etwas kaltem Wasser aufgelöst, bringe es über Kohlenfeuer und quirle es so lange scharf, bis es aufkochen will, worauf man es schnell vom Feuer nimmt, den Rahm noch so lange rührt, bis er kalt wird, und bereitet die Pasteten sofort wie gewöhnlich.

25. Gänseleberpastete (Gooseliver pie).

6 große, weiße Gänselebern werden mit feingeschnittenem Speck und frischen Trüffeln gespickt und mit Provenceröl, Kräuterpulver und Citronensaft marinirt, dann nimmt man ½ Pfund Trüffeln, ½ Pfund gekochtes Kalbfleisch oder einige Hühnerbrüste, ¼ Pfund Speck und etwas Charlottenzwiebeln und zerhackt alles fein, rührt ¼ Pfund Butter mit zwei Eiern gut ab, thut das Gehackte mit etwas Salz und 1 Pint Fleischbrühe dazu, rührt alles gut durch einander und stellt es bei Seite.

Nun wird ein beliebiger Pastetenteller mit Blätterteig belegt, der Boden desselben mit Parmesankäse bestreut, die Hälfte der obigen Fülle darüber gestrichen, dann die marinirte Gänseleber darauf, und hierauf die andere Hälfte der Fülle aufgetragen, diese mit dünnen Speckscheiben belegt und alles mit einem Deckel von Blätterteig bedeckt, solcher mit Eigelb bestrichen und nun die Pastete gebacken. Dieselbe ist ganz vorzüglich von Geschmack.

26. Gänseleberpastete, nachgeahmte, Gooseliver pie, imitated.

2 Pfund Kalbfleisch vom Schlegel, ½ Pfund frischer Speck, ein Stück von einer abgekochten geräucherten Ochsenzunge, oder auch Schinken, 1 Unze gewässerte ausgegrätete Sardellen, 2 Eßlöffel Kapern, das Mark und die Schale einer Citrone, dies alles wird fein gehackt, dann mit Cardamom, Muskatblüthe, Nelken und Pfeffer gewürzt und in einer Schüssel mit 4 Löffel Wein gut durch einander gerührt. Mit dieser Mischung wird der Pastetenteig gefüllt und gebacken.

27. Aalpastetchen (Eel patty).

Die Hülle oder Form besteht aus Blätterteig. Es werden von dem reinen Aalfleische eines gut abgelegenen Aales dünne, abgerundete Stücke geschnitten und diese, nach dem Einsalzen, in Butter, feinen Kräutern und Citronensaft steif gemacht.

Von allen Fischabfällen, Kräuterbutter, Sardellen=
butter, Parmesankäse, einem guten Theil dicker, brauner Fleischbrühsauce und Semmelbrei bereitet man eine so feine Füllung, daß eine Probe davon auf der Zunge zer=
fällt. Dann sticht man von dem zu etwa $\frac{1}{4}$ Zoll dick ausgerollten Teige mit einem Ausstecher Böden aus von etwa 6 Zoll im Durchmesser, bestreicht sie mit Ei, umgiebt die äußere Oberfläche mit einem schmalen, $\frac{1}{2}$ Zoll hohen Kranze, thut in die Mitte etwas Farce, dann ein Aalstück und wieder Farce, so daß es eine erhabene Form giebt, bestreut es, mit besonderer Beachtung, daß nichts auf den Teigrand falle, mit Parmesankäse, be=
träufelt es mit Krebs= oder anderer Butter, bestreicht den Teigrand mit Ei, wobei nichts an den Seiten über=
fließen darf, und backt die Pastetchen in scharfer Hitze. Man kann diese Pasteten auch aus zwei Teigböden herstellen.

28. Austernpastetchen (Oyster patty).

Die Hülle besteht aus Blätterteig, und die übrige Bereitung ist gleich der vorstehenden.

In eine äußerst feine Farce kommt auch die kurzge=
kochte Austernbrühe, welche von den Austern, die in Rheinwein steif gemacht worden, zurückgeblieben ist. Statt dieser Farce, wie sie bei den Aalpasteten angegeben

ist, macht man auch eine von geriebener Semmel, fein geschnittenen Kräutern, Sardellenbutter, einigen Eiern, Butter und etwas Rheinwein, und legt in jede Pastete zwischen die Farce 3 vom Bart befreite Austern. Auch die Austernpastetchen kann man aus zwei Teigböden machen.

29. Krebspastetchen (Crabfish patty).

Man nimmt dazu Blätterteig, den man dünn ausrollt, und belegt damit kleine Pastetenförmchen, oder man bereitet die Hülle ebenso wie bei den Aalpastetchen.

Dann bereitet man von 1½ Quart Milch, 4 Eiern, die man mit 2 Löffeln voll Mehl, einem reichlichen ¼ Pfund Krebsbutter, 2 Unzen Zucker und etwas Muskatnuß auf dem Feuer abrührt, eine Masse; und wenn dieselbe kalt ist, so rührt man sie gut mit 6 Eidottern und zieht zuletzt das zu Schnee geschlagene Weiße von 4 Eiern darunter. In jede der Pastetenförmchen thut man nun ½ Löffel feines Krebsragout hinein, welches man mit Parmesankäse und Krebsbutter deckt und mit der obigen Masse überzieht, so daß die Förmchen ziemlich voll werden.

30. Preiselbeerenpastete (Cranberry pie).

Koche 1 Pfund Preiselbeeren mit 1 Pint Wasser weich, thue 1 Pfund feinen weißen Zucker hinzu und laß es noch 15 bis 20 Minuten gelinde kochen.

Eine andere Art. Koche 1 Pfund Preiselbeeren mit 1 Quart Wasser weich, thue 1 Pfund Zucker dazu, mische 1 Unze Cornstarch mit etwas kaltem Wasser an und gieße sie, wenn es wieder im Kochen ist, hinein, laß es noch 1 bis 2 Minuten kochen und nimm es vom Feuer.

31. Aprikosenpastete (Apricot pie).

2 Pfund Aprikosen werden geschält, von den Steinen befreit, in 4 Stücke geschnitten, mit 1 Unze geriebener süßen Mandeln, ¼ Unze bitteren Mandeln, ¼ Pfd. Zucker, ¼ Unze Citronat, der abgeriebenen Schale einer Citrone, ¼ Unze gemischtem Gewürz, nebst so viel Hausenblase, daß die Masse gallern kann, gekocht, nach dem Erkalten die Pasteten damit ausgefüllt und gebacken wie gewöhnlich.

32. Ananaspastete (Pine apple pie).

Schäle die Ananas, schneide sie in dünne Scheiben, mische sie in einem Kessel mit Zucker, abgeriebener Citronenschale, gestoßenem Zimmt und etwas Rheinwein, und schmore sie ein wenig über gelindem Feuer, ehe die Pasteten damit gefüllt werden.

33. Citronen-Rahmpastete (Lemon cream pie).

Man rührt zu 10 Eidottern 1 Unze Mehl oder Cornstarch, den Saft und die abgeriebene Rinde von 4 Citronen, ½ Pfund Zucker, 4 Unzen geriebene Mandeln, unter welchen 1 Unze bittere sind, 2 Unzen Citronat, etwas Cardamom, ½ Pint Rheinwein und etwas Salz, bringt alles über das Feuer und rührt es so lange, bis es recht heiß und etwas dick wird, und mischt den Schnee von der Hälfte des Eiweises darunter.

34. Früchtepastete von getrockneten Früchten (Fruit pie of dried Fruits).

Alle Arten getrockneter Früchte, als wie Pfirsiche, Aepfel, New York Plums, Prunes u. s. w., müssen erst eine Zeit lang in Wasser geweicht werden, und koche sie dann bei gelindem Feuer recht weich; reibe sie durch einen Durchschlag, thue den Zucker hinzu und laß sie noch so lange kochen, bis alles Wasser ziemlich eingekocht ist und die Masse der Früchtebutter gleich sieht.

Drittes Kapitel.

Von den verschiedenen Eierrahmen (Custards).

Allgemeine Bemerkungen.

Zum Eierrahm gebrauche man stets nur frische Eier. Man koche den Eierrahm immer in einem Kessel, der in einem Gefäße mit siedendem Wasser steht. Die Eier sollten nie in sehr heiße Milch gethan werden.

1. Gekochter Eierrahm (Boiled Custard).

Koche 1 Quart Milch mit ein wenig ganzem Zimmt und etwas Citronenschale, versüße sie mit 1½ Pfund feinem weißen Zucker, seihe sie ab, und wenn sie sich ein wenig abgekühlt hat, mische allmälig 8 gut zerschlagene

Eier und etwas Rosenwasser hinein. Rühre alles zusammen über einem gelinden Feuer, bis es die richtige Dicke hat, und gieße es dann in Tassen oder Gläser.

2. Eine andere Art.

Nimm das Gelbe von 6 Eiern und 4 ganze Eier, schlage sie mit ½ Pfund Zucker leicht, und mische sie allmälig zu einem Quart Milch, wenn sie beinahe am Sieden ist, füge etwas Rosenwasser hinzu und rühre alles so lange über gelindem Feuer, bis es die richtige Dicke hat, gieße es in Tassen oder Gläser, streiche den Schnee von dem zurückgebliebenen Eiweiß darüber, streue ganz feinen Zucker darauf und glacire es, indem man eine glühende Glacirschaufel oder ein anderes breites und starkes Eisen darüber hält.

3. Gewöhnlicher Eierrahm (Common Custard).

Siede 1 Quart Milch mit etwas ganzem Zimmt und Citronenschale, mische 1 Unze Cornstarch mit ein wenig kalter Milch, gieße die gekochte Milch durch ein Sieb darüber und rühre allmälig das wohl zerschlagene Gelbe von 6 Eiern hinzu. Bringe es wieder über das gelinde Feuer, rühre es so lange, bis es die rechte Dicke hat, gieße es in Tassen oder Gläser und siebe ein wenig feinen Zucker und Maskatnuß darüber.

4. Reis-Eierrahm (Rice Custard).

Mische ein Pint Milch, ein Pint Rahm, 1 Unze ge=
siebtes Reismehl, etwas Rosenwasser, ¼ Pfund Zucker
und rühre es auf dem Feuer so lange zusammen, bis es
anfängt zu kochen; oder koche 2 Unzen ganzen, rein ge=
lesenen Reis in 1 Quart Milch gut weich, rühre dann
das wohl zerschlagene Gelbe von 4 Eiern dazu und laß
es bei stetem Kochen noch einige Minuten gelinde kochen;
fülle es dann in Tassen und streue ein wenig feinen
Zucker und Muskatnuß darauf.

5. Gebackener Eierrahm (Baked Custard).

Schlage 12 Eier mit ¾ Pfund feinem weißen Zucker
recht leicht und gieße bei fortwährendem Schlagen zwei
Quart Milch langsam hinzu, nebst etwas Muskatnuß
und Rosenwasser, oder Zimmt und abgeriebener Citro=
nenschale. Belege die Teller mit Teig, setze sie in den
Ofen und fülle sie dann aus, doch nicht mehr als drei
Teller zu gleicher Zeit, weil sonst der Teig in den an=
dern Tellern Blasen zieht, ehe sie ausgefüllt werden
können.

6. Eine andere Art.

Siede 2 Quart Milch mit etwas Zimmt und Citro=
nenschale, mische 4 Unzen Cornstarch mit etwas kalter

Milch (ungefähr 1 Pint), gieße die kochende Milch durch ein Sieb darüber und, bei fortwährendem Umrühren, noch 2 Quart kalte Milch hinzu. Schlage 12 Eier mit 1 Pfund Zucker leicht, und bei immerwährendem Schlagen lasse die ganze Milch langsam dazu laufen, schlage alles zusammen noch einige Zeit und backe die Masse wie die obige.

7. Cocosnuß=Eierrahm (Cocoanut Custard).

Schlage 12 Eier mit 1 Pfund Zucker leicht zusammen, rühre 2 bis 4 Unzen geschmolzene und geklärte Butter, eine geschälte und geriebene Cocosnuß, nebst 2 Quart Milch langsam hinzu, schlage alles zusammen noch eine Zeit lang, und backe es wie gewöhnlich.

8. Eine andere Art.

Schlage 16 Eier mit 1 Pfund Zucker leicht, rühre 1 geriebene Cocosnuß, $\frac{1}{4}$ Pfund Butter und 2 Quart Milch langsam dazu; weiche 2 bis 3 Pfund Brod in 2 Quart Milch auf, reibe es durch einen Durchschlag und mische es unter die obige Masse, schlage alles zusammen noch einige Minten und backe die Custards wie gewöhnlich. Diese Masse eignet sich besonders gut für die kleinen Cocosnuß=Pasteten.

9. Kürbiß=Eierrahm (Pumpkin Custard).

Zerschneide einen Kürbiß in Stücke, befreie dieselben von dem inneren Saamen und der äußeren Rinde, koche 8 Pfund von dem Mark recht weich, gieße es in einen Durchschlag und laß das Wasser gut ablaufen, reibe es durch in einen Topf, rühre ¼ Pfund Butter, ½ Unze Salz, 2 Unzen gemahlenen Ingwer (ginger), etwas abgeriebene Citronenschale und 3 Quart Milch hinzu. Schlage 18 Eier mit 1½ Pfund Zucker recht leicht, mische alles gut zusammen und backe die Custards wie gewöhnlich.

10. Süße Kartoffel=Eierrahm (Sweet Potatoe Custard).

Koche 4 Pfund süße Kartoffeln (sei vorsichtig, daß keine kranke darunter ist, weil sonst alle danach schmecken), schäle sie und reibe sie durch einen Durchschlag, rühre ¼ Pfund Butter, etwas Zimmt und 2 Quart Milch, nebst 8 Eiern, mit ½ Pfund Zucker leicht gerührt, hinzu, schlage alles zusammen noch einige Minuten und verfahre damit wie bei den vorigen Custards.

11. Käse=Eierrahm (Cheese Custard).

Weiche 1 Pfund Brod in 1 Quart Milch, und reibe es mit 4 Pfund süßem Käse durch einen Durchschlag, schlage 12 Eier mit 1 Pfund Zucker recht leicht, und gieße 2 Quart Milch langsam hinzu, rühre alles gut zusammen, nebst etwas Zimmt, abgeriebener Citronen= schale und ein wenig Rosenwasser, und backe die Cu= stards wie gewöhnlich.

Inhaltsverzeichniss.

—•✠✠•—

Erstes Kapitel.

———

Von den verschiedenen, im Geschäfte des amerikanischen
Pastetenbäckers vorkommenden Backwerken.

Zweites Kapitel.

———

Von der Zubereitung der Pasteten, Torten und ihrer
verschiedenen Füllungen.

Drittes Kapitel.

Von den verschiedenen Eierrahmen (Custard).

The American

PASTRY BAKER.

In English and German.

BY

FR. OTTO,

Practical Pastry Baker.

PUBLISHED BY

Hoffman & Morwitz, 612 & 614 Chestnut Street,

PHILADELPHIA.

www.ingramcontent.com/pod-product-compliance
Lightning Source LLC
Chambersburg PA
CBHW020237090426
42735CB00010B/1725